CHASING the MOON'S SHADOW

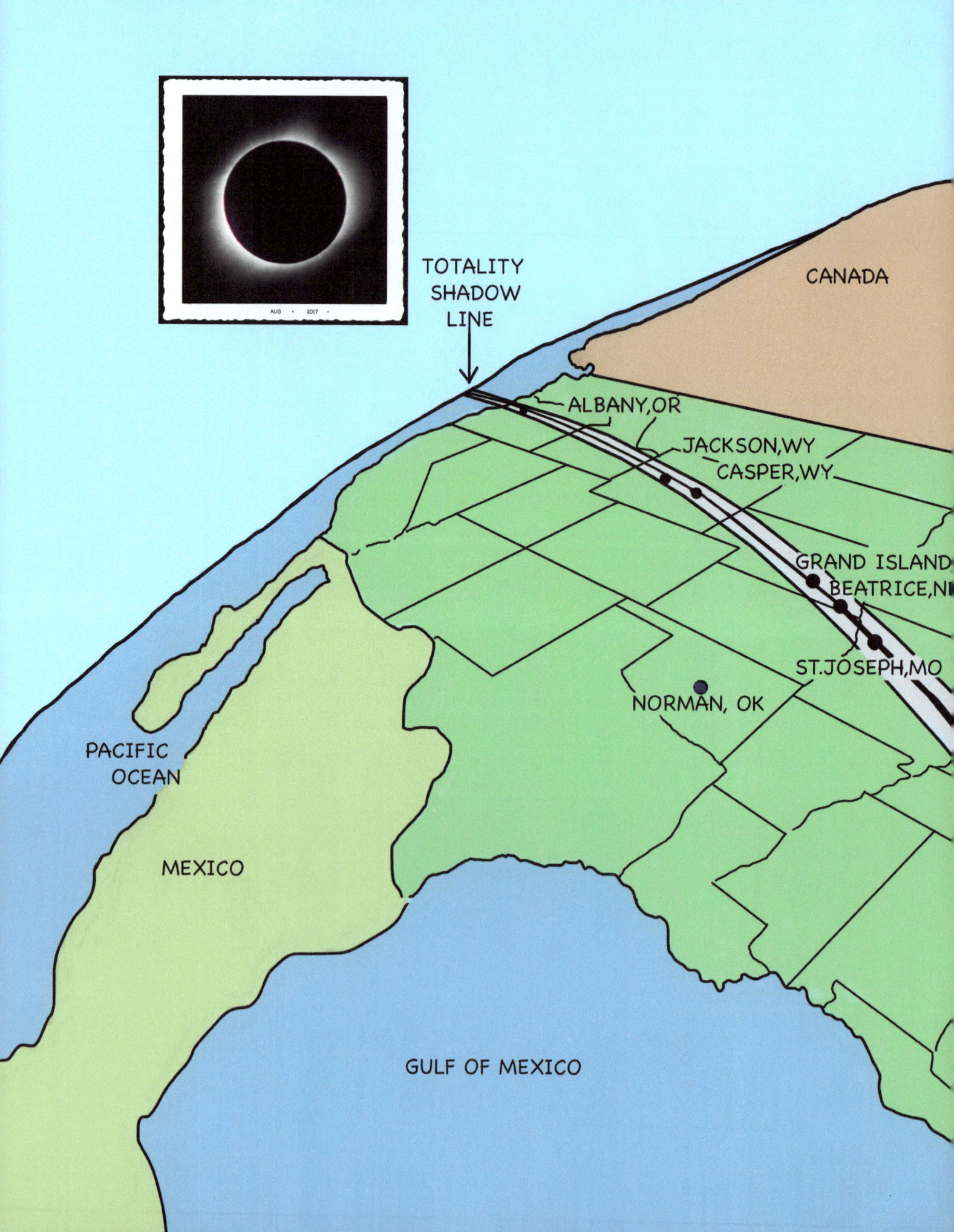

CHASING the MOON'S SHADOW

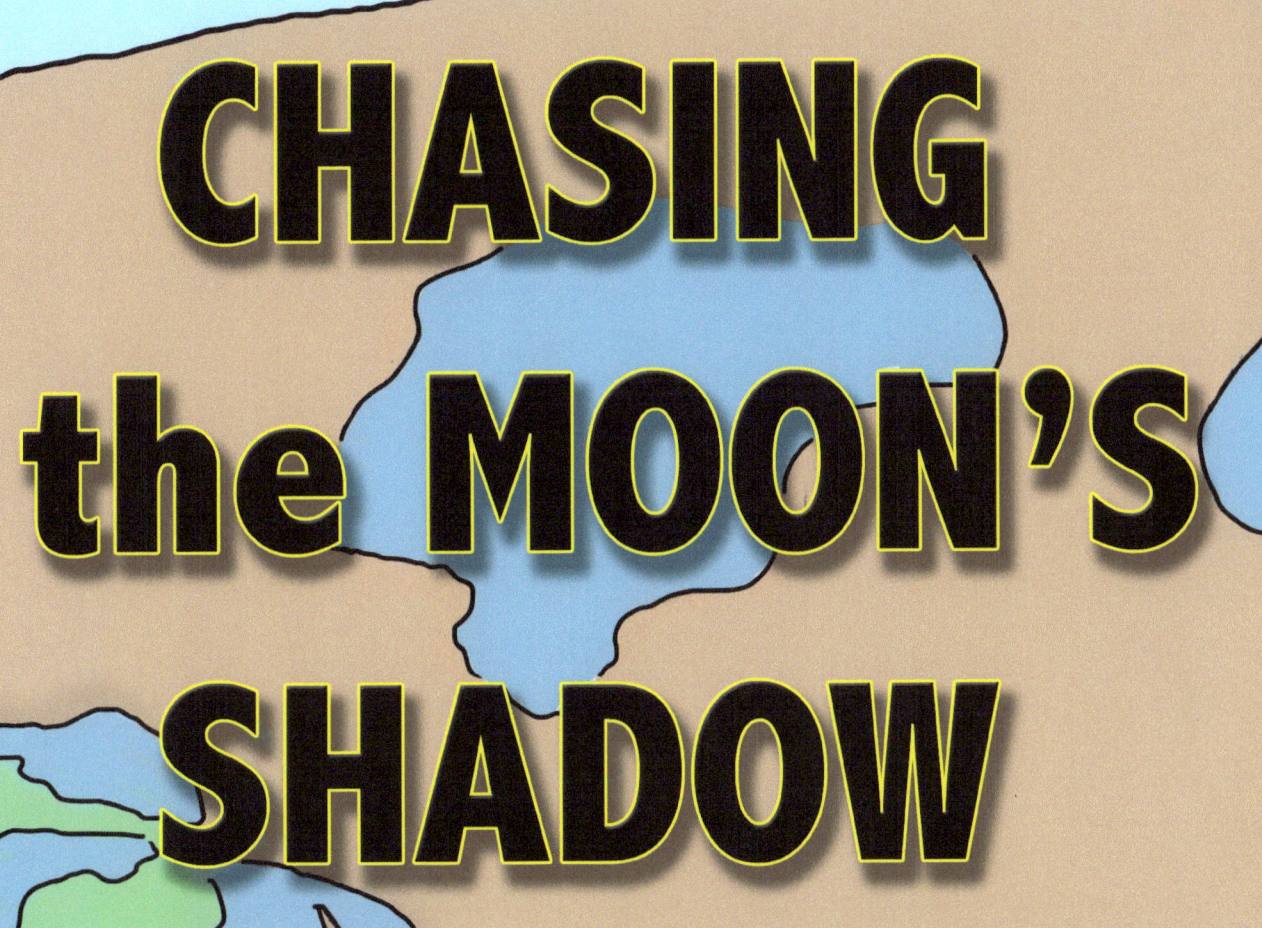

WRITTEN AND ILLUSTRATED BY
CAROLYN MACY
PHOTOGRAPHY BY JEREMY MACY

Dedicated to Daddy,
my family, and friends.

Chasing the Moon's Shadow
Copyright © 2018 by Carolyn Macy and Jeremy Macy. All rights reserved.

No part of this publication may be reproduced, stored in a retrieval system or transmitted in any way by any means, electronic, mechanical, photocopy, recording or otherwise without the prior permission of the author except as provided by USA copyright law.

Published by Carolyn Macy
6227 81st Avenue N.E. | Norman, Oklahoma 73026 USA
405.401.2012

Book design copyright © 2018 by Carolyn Macy.
Written and Illustrated by Carolyn Macy
Photographs by Jeremy Macy

Published in the United States of America
ISBN: 978-1-7328604-0-7 (Softcover) 987-1-7328604-1-4 (Hardcover)
987-1-7328604-2-1 (ebook)
LCCN: 2018910228
1. JUVENILE NONFICTION / Biography & Autobiography
2. JUVENILE NONFICTION / Science & Nature / Astronomy

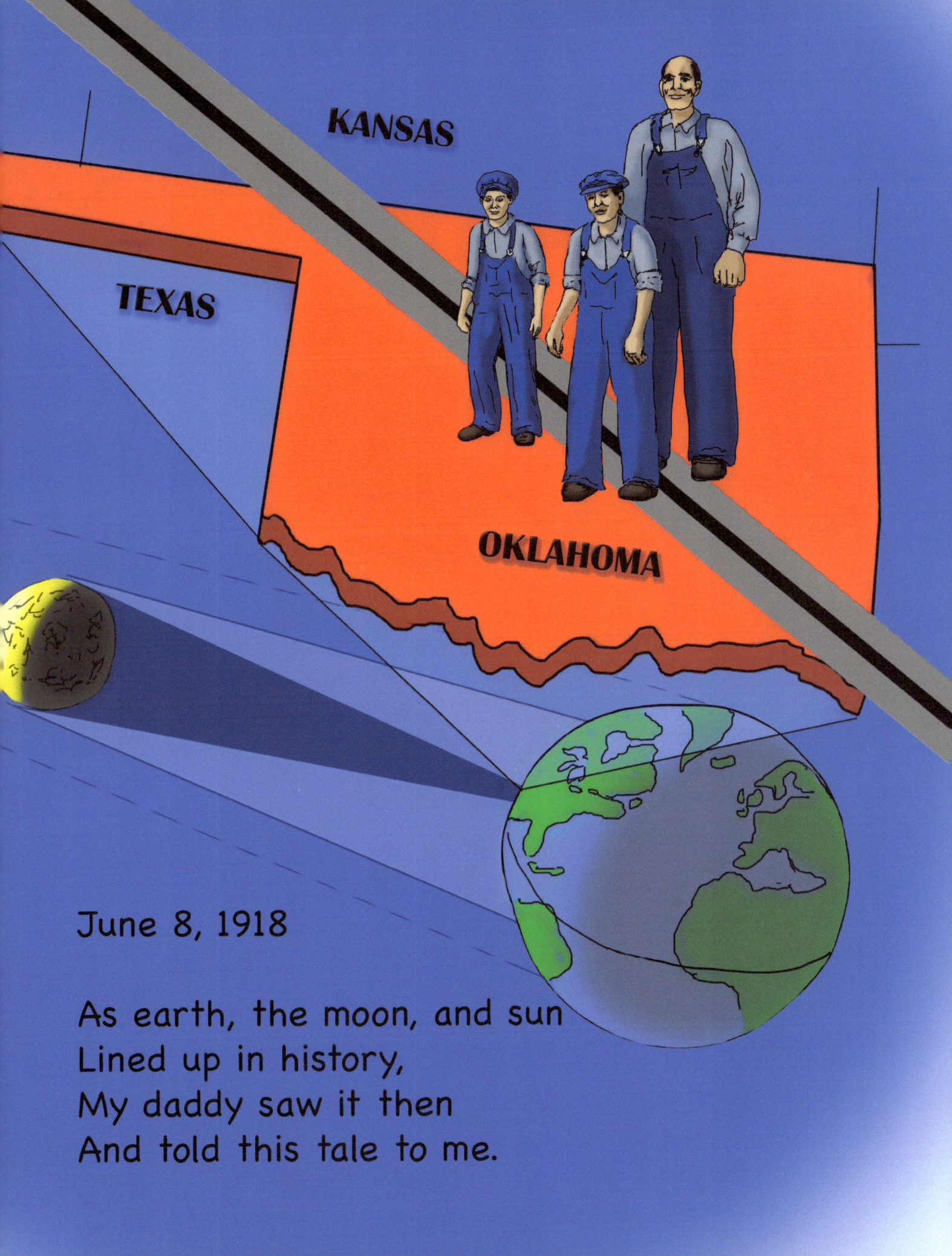

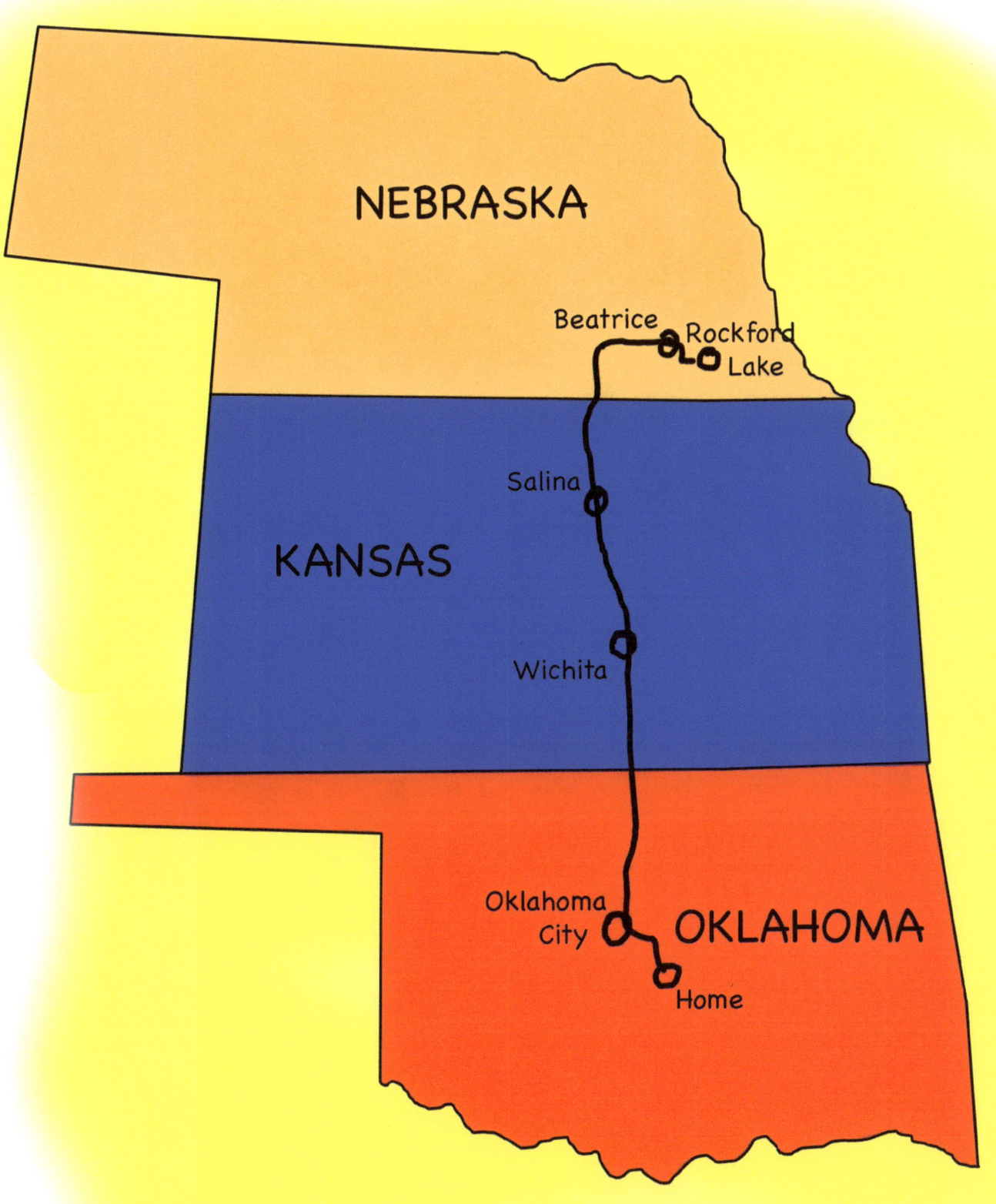

First north and then back east
To where we planned to stay.

We turned in after dark
To sleep 'til morning light,
But noises woke us up
To find a tent in flight.

Gale winds had ripped it up
And flung it down close by.
Our stuggle pushing back
Proved troublesome to try.

Another tent collapsed
To trap a child in it.
We rushed to pull him free
As heavy rainfall hit.

The wind picked up the tent
And wrapped it all around
With such a mighty force,
It knocked me to the ground.

August 20, 2017

The rain went on its way,
But left us wet and chilled.
Our camp we straightened up
Since stormy winds had stilled.

All crowded into cars
To sleep 'til morning rose,

Then found a Laundromat
For drying rain-soaked clothes.

(approximate Totality:
2 minute 34 seconds)

Corona's fiery ring
Emerged in dazzling sight.
We stood in frozen awe
While daytime turned to night.

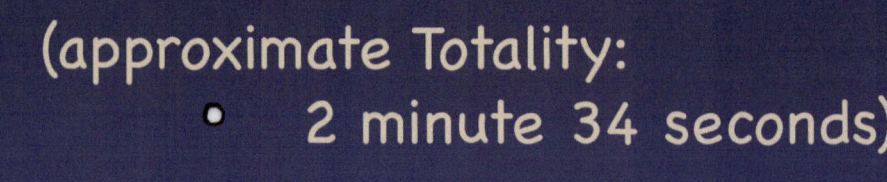

A brilliant sunset sky
Encircled all around.
The sunset and eclipse,
We watched without a sound.

The moon chased on its way
To let the sun shine out.
A normal day returned
As crowds moved on about.

www.ingramcontent.com/pod-product-compliance
Lightning Source LLC
Chambersburg PA
CBHW041120070526
44584CB00002B/221